P9-BZO-875

3 3484 00141 8547

From Blossom to Fruit

by

Gail Saunders-Smith

Pebble Books

an imprint of Capstone Press

1

Pebble Books

Pebble Books are published by Capstone Press
818 North Willow Street, Mankato, Minnesota 56001
http://www.capstone-press.com
Copyright © 1998 by Capstone Press

All Rights Reserved • Printed in the United States of America

Library of Congress Cataloging-in-Publication Data
Saunders-Smith, Gail.
    From blossom to fruit/by Gail Saunders-Smith.
        p. cm.
    Includes bibliographical references (p. 23) and index.
    Summary: Simple text and photographs describe the growth
of an apple from blossom to ripe fruit.
    ISBN 1-56065-584-4
    1. Apples--Development--Juvenile literature. [1. Apples.]
I. Title.

SB363.S284 1998
634'.11--dc21
                                    97-29803
                                        CIP
                                        AC

Editorial Credits
Lois Wallentine, editor; Timothy Halldin and James Franklin,
design; Michelle L. Norstad, photo research

Photo Credits
William D. Adams, 4
Dwight Kuhn, 12, 14
John Marshall Outdoor Photography, cover, 20
Unicorn Stock/Judy Hile, 6; Frank Pennington, 8; Joseph
    Fontenot, 16; Martha McBride, 1, 18
Willowbrook Photography/Ken Weidenbach, 10

Table of Contents

Dwight Foster Public Library
102 East Milwaukee Ave.
Fort Atkinson, WI 53538

4

These pink blossoms
are closed.

These white blossoms
have opened.

Blossoms have
five white petals.

Bees visit blossoms.

The petals fall off.

A tiny fruit forms.

The apples grow.

The apples turn
red or green or yellow.

The apples are
ready to be picked.

Words to Know

bee—an insect that collects pollen from apple blossoms; this helps apple blossoms turn into fruit.

blossom—a flower on a fruit tree or other plant

fruit—the part of a plant that contains seeds and usually can be eaten

petal—one of the outer parts of a blossom or a flower

Read More

Burckhardt, Ann L. *Apples.* Mankato, Minn.: Bridgestone Books, 1996.

Gibbons, Gail. *The Seasons of Arnold's Apple Tree.* San Diego: Harcourt Brace Jovanovich, 1984.

Micucci, Charles. *The Life and Times of the Apple.* New York: Orchard Books, 1992.

Internet Sites

Apple Facts: How Do You Grow Apples?
http://www.pref.aomori.jp/nourin/ringo/rin-e06.html

Healthy Choices for Kids
http://www.healthychoices.org

UVM Apple Orchard
http://orchard.uvm.edu/uvmapple/default.html

Note to Parents and Teachers

This book describes the stages of an apple's development from blossom to fruit. The text and photographs enable young children to see and understand how one stage leads to the next. The clear photographs support the beginning reader in making and maintaining the meaning of the text. Children may need assistance in using the Table of Contents, Words to Know, Read More, Internet Sites, and Index/Word List sections of the book.

Index/Word List

Word Count: 44
Early-Intervention Level: 10

24